The Torah Garden

The
Torah
Garden

Philip Terman

Autumn House
Press

PITTSBURGH

"Autumn House" and "Autumn House Press" are registered trademarks owned by Autumn House Press, a nonprofit corporation whose mission is the publication and promotion of poetry and other fine literature.

Autumn House Press Staff

Editor-in-Chief and Founder: Michael Simms
Executive Director: Richard St. John
Co-Founder: Eva-Maria Simms
Managing Editor: Adrienne Block
Community Outreach Director: Michael Wurster
Fiction Editors: Sharon Dilworth, John Fried, Stewart O'Nan
Associate Editors: Ziggy Edwards, Erik Rosen, Rebecca King
Designers: Kathy Boykowycz, Chiquita Babb, Rebecca King
Media Consultant: Jan Beatty
Publishing Consultant: Peter Oresick
Technology Consultant: Evan Oare
Tech Crew Chief: Michael Milberger
Interns: D. Gilson, Caroline Tanski

PENNSYLVANIA COUNCIL ON THE ARTS   Autumn House Press receives state arts funding support through a grant from the Pennsylvania Council on the Arts, a state agency founded by the Commonwealth of Pennsylvania and the National Endowment for the Arts, a federal agency.

ISBN: 978-1-932870-51-0

Library of Congress Control Number:

for Malka

I will give the rains of your land
in its season, the former rain
and the latter rain, that thou
mayest gather corn, and thy wine
and thine oil. And I will give grass
in thy fields for thy cattle and thou
shalt eat and be satisfied.

Deuteronomy 11: 14-15

Contents

Three

Four: *The Torah Garden*

The Torah Garden

Among the Unspoken Names

We would be like the old Jews,
who knew nothing but devotion and gratitude,
every word was praise, praise, praise,

their bodies as the wind, their lives a poverty, their spirits everything,
everything they spoke sang of creation,
their stomachs empty, lips parched, eyes hungry for the text—

the world was nowhere, even in summer,
even as the apples rounded and the quick birds flew
their quick flights from branch to branch,

even as sunlight spread itself, even dusk,
nothing could sway them outside those pages
to which they swayed.

We would be like the old sages—
for whom it was God this and God that,
nothing was as it was, everything was something else,
that blue jay, that grass, not blue only, not green only—

move closer, closer to the garden, how it floats under the illuminated
    sky, softer, softer,
into that obscure place—

be nothing but an ear, they said.
Have you made arrangements, they asked,

about this hour, such as it is,
this hour of ecstasy and service, this document of mid-summer,
these days of drought and resurrection—

we would be like them,
we would turn into the book completely,
we would walk around the garden seven times
out of some obscure longing
we would ask our ancestors to explain,

we would be like the old interpreters,
whose words had wings,
we would climb the rungs of the ladder reaching up to the bird's nest,

if it weren't for the morning sleep and the midday wine and the
        children's talk—

we would be as those scribes,
scribbling our sixteen hours a day, tonguing the sweetness of the
        letters,
lost happily among the syllables—

if it weren't that we were stuck in the midst of all this beauty,
if it weren't for these children crouched in the apple tree,
faces flushed like apples, voices shrieking like blue jays—

we would know that the Madonna lilies are not Madonna lilies only,
nor are the grapes their blood-purple, not their sweetness only...

Will our plantings flower as dust?
Will our tomatoes suffer again their blight?

Or will the corn stalks be as scrolls lifted out of their dwellings,
bearing their fruit as plentiful as words?

We would, we think, be among the blessed,
the unspoken names,

we would be among the stories passed down,

if it weren't that we wanted to sing the whole thing,
the flesh of the earth, the consuming flames.

one

Donning *Tefillin*

Years it's been since I retrieved
the long white-fringed *tallis*
and the black thick straps

out of the blue velvet pouch,
a Star of David sewn into its side,
secured with a zipper, that my mother

safeguarded in a special drawer
beside her mother's two brass candleholders
and hand-knit shawl.

Rev Lev, our synagogue sage,
the Rebbe of our restlessness,
short and paunchy, hunched over,

a little like a *schlemiel*, voice off-key
as he taught us our Torah portions
in the small chapel beneath the main

sanctuary, instructed us one by one
to recite those passages of the story
that corresponded with our birth.

My arm would tense and turn
slightly purple as the Rev softly
guided my hand, his thick fingers

manipulating mine as we strapped
and then unstrapped the binds
seven times until they revealed

the flushed impressions of spirals
along the length of my bare arm,
my skin slightly itching the way

it did, once, when the plaster cast
clasped around the broken bone, my arm
goose-pimpled, tiny hairs bristling,

my flesh burning to become a man.

Mandelstam Didn't Join My Grandfather

Mandelstam, why didn't you stay in Paris?
Or, better yet, why didn't you join
my grandfather when he boarded the ship

in 1906? Fifteen, before the "Dostoevskian
moments of scandal," before the words
about the fat worms and the cockroaches?

Then you could have, as he did, started
a family of heartbreak and scattered
your seed all across the suburbs

of the Midwest. And, instead of refusing,
in your captivity, for fear of poison,
the peels and the scraps, you could have,

like my grandfather, leaned
your exhausted body against the sink
after a long day of building houses

and spread the herring-in-wine-sauce
across the generous bread
and washed it down with a thimbleful of vodka.

Instead, you read Petrarch to the prisoners
by the fire. In happiness you didn't believe.
Instead of a small brown house

with yellow trim, you went to the camp
in your yellow coat, joking to the end.
Instead of your poems passed around from hand

to hand, mouth to mouth, sewn into cushions,
stuck inside saucepans and shoes,
instead of "we have done away with a great poet"—

they could have been silent
as the stars over the snows of Cleveland—
scattered to the winds, but *nothing*, you said,

can be completely scattered to the winds.
If someone has something to say,
you said, *he will always manage to say it.*

A History of America

Uncle Hy, 83 and failing, fumbling
with two remotes— one for the TV,
one for the VCR—static, then a game show,
then static again, then—he's still fiddling—

the opening scene for *Bonanza*, September 14, 1961—
and there he is again, in his prime, galloping
into town, all duded up, wavy black hair,
dark hat, striking as Grant and Gable

in his Hollywood handsome looks, save
for the elongated nose. After the war
he hauled boxes of soda pop off a truck.
Nights he ushered downtown

where he'd stare at all the enormous stars,
already a little famous in Cain Park productions
in Cleveland Heights, Ohio and at Corky
and Lenny's Delicatessen where he'd arrive

fully costumed for the laughs. He answered Cecil's ad
for a Jewish slave and drove out west
in a poor Ford. There was a clown stint
on a kid show and a lurpy hospital aid bit part

on the *Joey Bishop Hour* and he dated
Jerry Lewis' secretary. Now, on the screen,

his horse rides into town, halts,—he swings down
onto the dusty road in front of the saloon,

tough in silver-buttoned vest, Stetson,
bandana tucked below the chin,
clean face tinged with conniving. We watch
from his couch in this messy condominium

on Fulton Street near Ventura Boulevard.
Back hunched over, he's leaning, one hand
grasping his cane, eating slowly the Salisbury steak
from his meals-on-wheels dinner,

on the coffee table a stack of affidavits about
the ongoing lawsuit he's enmeshed in against
his second ex-wife who, he claims, after
he signed over power-of-attorney, took everything—

the houses, the money, the son, and remarried,
and now he can't afford the nursing home
he doesn't want to move into—he's approaching
an innocent woman, offering, with a sly grin,

to "escort" her, and she declines, politely,
and he comes closer, offers again in a voice
of false charm, and—suddenly, Hoss appears,
reliable white hat, inquires of the woman

in his low voice: "Need any help, Ma'am?"
"No, thank-you," she says with her voice but
"Yes, please," she says with her eyes, and
Uncle Hy tells Hoss to "butt out," swinging

his fist, and they fall into the dust, struggle,
and Uncle Hy takes out a gun, the camera
zooming in on the young woman's face,
which twitches when the shot explodes,

and we watch Uncle Hy's younger body
loosening, writhing, dying,
the theme song rising, the opening credits
rolling, his name not among them.

Lobsters

Mickey got me high for the first time
in the woods behind the parking lot
of The Lobster Pot, where we worked

our shifts. When customers
thinned out and the manager smoked
and drank at the bar with the waitresses,

we'd reach our hands into the cold
water of the tank, grab the back
of a hard shell, wooden pegs clamping

their claws, and place them on the carpet,
their alien bodies squirming and sliding
off-course, aimless in this strange element,

not like when our huge black cook
in the boiling kitchen would drop them
straight into the bubbling water.

"Hotter than hell in here," she'd shout,
chugging a dripping bottle of Stroh's,
as I lined dirty dish after dirty dish

onto the rack to be conveyed into
the machine, underage and overtime,
paid off the clock. Way past when

I was to call home for a ride, Mickey,
pockmarked, thick black hair greased back,
led me into the after-hour dark

through the few parked cars and into
the darker woods. I thought, toking in
this new freedom, of my parents

waiting by the phone, until we saw
the police car's headlights slicing
the night like swords, and Mickey

blending in with the blur, and I knew
a hand was lifting me above the impossible-
to-imagine next moment.

Three-Card Monte

I walked everywhere
on that island, an island myself,
twenty, just up from the Midwest,

ready to begin that long book
called my life, aimless, swayed
by whatever was at hand, strolling

blind. On 5th Avenue—a figure,
emaciated, barely distinguishable
in the skyscraper's shadow,

on the steaming sidewalk,
inside a circle of watchers. Above
his podium cardboard box

he flashed three cards—
two clubs and one heart—
the queen—then turned

them over and the quick slide,
hands gliding like acrobats,
the cards revolving around

and over and under and through
until they lost their shapes,
spinning like blades as if

by some inner force, a fast-
forward choreography.
I couldn't keep my eyes off

what I was sure to be the queen,
the one to watch, certain
if I held her attention

it would prove something
I needed, what I had to master,
this street preacher staring

straight into my eyes,
whispering, voice like gravel:
a twenty will get you a hundred—

and I was confident in the heart
I tracked, staked my savings
on what my eyes stalked.

Of course I was wrong.
And I returned to the Midwest
where I had to start again

from scratch, following
in my mind the movement
of those cards and the brilliant

fingers that manipulated them
until they became a blur, like that city
I'm not certain was there at all.

The Tool Shop

Ten hours a day the same motion.

Fists clenched against the double press,
I release the tension
and steel bits drill through black iron.

Behind plated glass,
the boss watches us
make love to our machines.

I rack each bar to George,
crew cut and seventy,
who fits two smaller bars into holes
with hands that quiver from the grip
of fifty years.

Bar, lock-in-press, release—
each hole has to be centered—
bar, lock-in-press, release…

a black iron bar with holes off-center
shakes feverishly in George's hand,
as if he would knock me cold,
and I return.

What are we making?
Toilet wrenches?

George, you're dying
from lighting your next non-filter
with your last, and I'm drifting so far
he'll have to lay me off.

Oil City Serenade

I want to sing to you, Oil City,
home of artist Butch Quinn who is drinking a beer
at midnight and drawing figures on canvas
with cigarette ash—muralist of refrigerators
dumped into the woods, the artist of logs left
by the sawmill, you'll find him at The Brass Rail
ogling the single mothers back in college,
abused and abandoned, their exes steal their tires
and hotwire their engines: town of despair,
let's paint you gray, let's shimmy on down
to the dollar store where on the racks are the royal robes
worn by every citizen. Let's sing the laid-off song,
the downsize song, the song that says we're going south,
sorry, let's sing the welfare romp. Let's do
Jake's Antiques, the old men behind the counter
sitting on torn leather chairs and smoking, staring
out of the dusty window at the line forming
in front of the Pennsylvania Lottery—one of them
a few years back actually won big, and has been in
and out of jail ever since—let's collect lottery tickets
and beer caps and cigarette butts and the smoke
that floats through the air. Let's open an account
of what we've lost: Quaker State, Continental Can,
Pittsburgh Steel, all of the hospital but the Mental Health Unit,
let's line up all the Prozac pills like coins along
the Petroleum Bridge and offer our naked bodies
to the telemarketing companies and Wal-Mart.

Once we were a city of Rockefellers.
Once we bled our earth out of its sweet juices.
Let's walk down to where the water cuts the town
in half, shielded from the sharp beams of Route 8
that glow like searchlights now that dusk seeps
beyond the hills steep as walls pushed back against
boarded-up buildings and dead-end streets.
Smell grease in the air, chemicals floating
like wounded birds from the one refinery left,
and if that goes, we're done.

    *

But have you lost yourself
in a late morning fog
for a good while as it breaks
apart slowly above the hills?

Have you smelled the matron
of the Polish Restaurant sweating,
balancing dishes of pierogies
steaming in the sauerkraut air?

Have you heard the soiled smoke
in Kirk Webb's voice
as he slides his lumber-yard fingers
up and down the after-hours strings
of his Silvertone, demonstrating
once again the resurrection
of Robert Johnson?

Has the corner of your eye
caught, in the twilight where
the river forks, a bald eagle
floating into the blurred edges?

Have you heard Evelyn Green,
small gray head under black beret,
shuffling her ninety-five years,
mumbling brilliant remarks
about Zen Buddhism?

Have you dreamed of the synagogue
hovering over the town like a one-winged angel?

Like a floating Talmudic page?

*

It's all the old people,
they say, and it's true,
you see them everywhere,

hobbling across the streets
at the appropriate lights,
staring out windows late,

writing letters to the editor
about the town cannon
and Lord save our hospital.

Saturdays it's bingo and Sundays
it's church, every other Friday
The Belles Lettres Club

with its strawberry cake
and instant coffee.
Their children have vanished

and disappeared south or west
in search of perpetual employment
and a day's worth of clean air.

The old are lined like the trees.
They pass like the shadows of hills
at dusk over the river.

*

Town with a river through your heart,
you know what they say of you:

quaker state gone   *hospital gone*   *youth gone*
charred lungs
makes you want to wash your hands

We, too, are bodies falling apart,
abandoned by our youth,
squeezed dry of our juices.

Who of us doesn't feel
like your sidewalks buckling
or your vacant buildings
boarded up and contemplating
their own dust?

　　　　*

I want to sing to you, Oil City—

The windows of Electralloy Steel
glare out at the black river

meaning the workers are punched in
and the sky will greet travelers

driving in on Route 8 out of Franklin
with handfuls of smoke rising

like gray balloons to the stars
we can no longer see or name.

When the oil executive out of New York
moved in with his wife,

she smelled the greasy air
and broke down and cried. But

on a Sunday night, the snow sparkling
like silver coins above the empty blocks,

lights off in the living rooms, you can almost
believe again in the old magical formula

of how oil equals money equals Victorian
mansions equal comfort. The derricks

and other creatures not found in nature
have disappeared into the imaginations

of dead capitalists. All the trees
have shed their soot, the railroad

has rolled up its rails for the night
and we are all working hard in the dark,

dreaming of wind blowing away smoke,
of Orion letting down his sword and belt.

Furnace and Shrine

Inside the narrow opening we stare up
through hemlock needles at the sky,
a winter blue tinged with late afternoon orange

after this, the worst blizzard in the history
of Western Pennsylvania: work's off, stores
shut down, even the reliable Interstate closed

east of Grove City all the way to the coast,
one hundred and some dead and still counting.
I followed as we trudged knee-deep through snow,

still accumulating, to the waterfall, frozen in air
except for what breaks through and rushes between
ice crusts to the Allegheny. We hiked along the stream,

one deliberate boot-step at a time, to what you call
this Mayan monument, dug deep into the hillside, built
from rough stone dressed at the edges, block by block

charred by the raw wood extracted like magic
from chestnut and oak that filled this country until
swallowed by the money monsters, or so would claim

the neighbors of Christian Myers and Henry Bear,
after they moved in with intentions: developers,
they called themselves, and the natives turned away

their faces, allowed them their bones for soup, ground
down, cooked over. Before the entrance we kneeled
on our hands and knees and grabbed hold and slid

slipping into the bosh, the interior, the hearth,
the womb, you chanted, my earth creature,
drawn to tunnels and caves, you know the secret openings,

the chambers where you'd sit in silence for hours,
snowed in, boiling water on the woodstove to bathe.
You go down underground, to the roots if you have to.

We try to stand where they blasted away with pistons and drums
the non-essentials, one layer fuel, one layer ore,
what they called *charges*, the way we strip down the dross

and the dirt until the molten metal oozes and seeps
in fire and exits out the four notches of the soul.
I could tell you the chronicle, how one ton iron required

three tons ore, how all the furnaces combined fifty tons
a week during the halcyon days, the pig metal transported
in flatboats to Pittsburgh, the wages good.

I could tell you production and profits, how in the end
they all failed, abandoned in the panic:
We need the necessary amount of flux, you say,

hands smoothing the firebrick, *to become fluid.*

Job Description

Isn't it my job to loaf and lean at the table,
to nap at inconvenient hours?
Aren't I getting paid to speak
inappropriately, to remain silent
when pressed, to avoid meetings?
Would you rather me be punctual?
When the snow arrives, I'm paid
to stick out my tongue. When
the light bulb shatters, my task
is to describe the dark. Don't expect me
to always return to the same chair
like a dog to the same tin bowl
in the corner of the kennel. I sleep
when others are awake, am awake
when others sleep. Hunger
is the most important ingredient
in my diet. When you point
to a plane, I'm staring at the moon.
When you point to the moon,
I'm digging the earth with my teeth.
I'll sign your petition with my epic.
Don't follow me unless you want
to go somewhere else. Don't
be surprised if I respond
to your chastisement
with an embrace. Or if I claim
paradise from my dung heap.
Or if I continue to talk long after
the wind has spoken its last elegy.

Two Geese

The two geese on the pond
will not stop their *kvetching*,
reminding me of my father

and my Aunt Sylvia when
one of them would throw
down a gin rummy hand

and the other would say:
"I can't play with you,"
and they'd both walk away,

only to return back
to their Pall Malls and scotch
and the only game

that could save them.
Sylvia was the gin rummy champion
of the Senior Citizen Division

at the Cleveland Jewish Center,
and she could belt out,
behind the ice-cream counter,

her cap barely balanced
on her fierce red hair,
a perfectly pitched aria.

Last time I saw her,
she was at the nursing home,
dying of cancer,

her voice like sandpaper
shuffling against
the trapped air:

This is hell, she said,
and I believed her.

Think of David and His Pleadings

So what if we return to the same theme
again and again—think of David
and his pleadings, think of Solomon
with his grandiose schemes, think
of Jehovah himself with his continual threats
and punishments, his promises and his
disappointments—so what if I return
to my family gathered around the set table,
waiting for my father, still in the backyard
examining the tomatoes in his garden
shadowed by the garage, how each evening
he'd return from his ten-hour-a-day labor
and water them, craving his small portion
of seed after the hours of asphalt and steel,
blaring horns and burning tires, so what
if he wanted, after punching out, the smell
of soil and grass staining his hands, greased
from all-day oil, or, if he needed, after the deals,
some silence from the complaints and excuses,
the dust and exhaust of Cleveland, the sweat—
so what if I return to the soft and delicate skins
he'd slice through—think of Moses
and his ultimatum—and eat, with a little salt.

11:11

Uncanny, how often I glance
at the digital clock flaring: *11:11,*

a symmetry of ones, lines stretching
toward the sky, pulling down into the earth—

the date my father died, veteran
of the second great war,

the last one, they say, worthy
of the fight, and then the aftermath:

wife and four sons, the daily grind
of coffee and work and supper: *11:11,*

reminding me of him, of something
he wants me to accomplish in his name,

saying, in the repetition of our loneliest
number: *I'm still here,* the number

out of which all other numbers arise:
one and *one* and *one* and *one,* what

some say the Lord is and what we remain
despite our efforts to lose ourselves in another,

what is divisible by only itself: 11:11,
a family of selves, each a single entity—

perhaps that, each of us is one more
than nothing—is that it?—the message

you send, from wherever you are, into time?
Or is the first of our infinity of odd numbers

just another one of your jokes, which
I'm reminded of when I'm reminded of you:

it's 11:11, and you're pushing up daisies.

The Last Torah Reader

has taken his voice—
more of a croak than a croon—
and his wisdom of the letters—

to chant among the sages.
He wasn't a learned man,
a laborer, rather,

just another lay member
of the congregation,
that became, in the absence

of a real rabbi, a shaman
of the secret signs
and mysterious marks

of the Masoretic text—
the accents and *nigguns*
and tropes, saying,

like a bearded *chazizan*
trained across the centuries,
each syllable according to its ritual,

the accents and intonations,
deciphering the florid vowel-less script,
swaying us through the service

in spite of ourselves.
He was our Ezra, as described
in the Book of Nehemiah, chanting

as if we just returned from exile,
taking on the obligation
that passed from tongue to tongue

for who knows how long,
performing the required *mitzvah*,
guiding our illiterate souls

in that week's portion of law.
We'd rise and he'd bellow
those passages from the open scroll:

off-key, out of tune, surging
beyond the sanctuary and across
the street. One of the Greatest Generation,

he was among those who liberated Dachau:
They had nowhere to go, he grieved,
then he returned to Butler, Pennsylvania

to commence his long marriage
and home improvement business
and good citizenship because for such

a position the chief qualification
is a measureless spirit, resounding
in his cracked voice our word of God.

two: To a Scientist Dying Young

For Bruce Israel Terman

Smart lad, to slip betimes away
From fields where glory does not stay,
And early though the laurel grows
It withers quicker than the rose.

A. E. Housman

The Accident

For the first four hours after
the accident you were John Doe,
anonymous as before your birth,

your great accomplishment unknown—
the discovery of a receptor
and its role in angiogenesis,

the inhibition of which may be
one strategy for treating cancer—
meaning it wasn't in the lexicon until

you found it and became the first
to so identify it, this presence that
arose out of nothing, or, not nothing,

as surely it was there for all to see
if they, like you, simply knew where
to look, like gravity or $E=mc^2$, and

all those other revelations beyond
my conception. Normally shy
and unassuming, you were effusive

explaining your triumph, drawing
diagrams on Starbucks napkins,
your face glowing with the ardor

of your occupation, and, more than
the equations, it's the groping I grasped,
as in poetry, the way in their invisibilities

these words wait for me to find them.
Now you're a body without a name,
removed from your relations,

in that place, perhaps, we return to
in sleep, but deeper, before knowledge,
or where all knowledge resides.

For those first few hours
you were as if under water,
or beyond the most visible star,

where not even your strongest lens
could locate you. Did you make
your greatest discoveries, the cures

to which all of your results
had been leading? And what journal
would publish them to the world?

Soon they identified you,
called the appropriate loved ones,
and your death began.

Washing the Body

I wanted to wash my brother's body,
the way he washed mine, as children,
in the bath, squeaking and splashing,
his older hands soaping my tender skin.

I wanted to touch him one last time,
not the way I brushed his chest
when he lay exposed in his injury,
his breath rising and falling

to the rhythm of the machines—
but rather to anoint with wet cloth
his freckled face, around his blue eyes
and small mouth, to work my way down

the shoulders and chest and stomach,
sponge his thighs and the hairs
we both inherited from our father
and from his father all the way back

to our first hairy father, and so
I am cleansing them, too, if what we are
is some portion of what others leave,
and I wanted, while reciting

he must depart as he came in,
to clean his nails and brush

his hair and to sprinkle holy soil
onto his flesh and place broken pottery

on his eyes, to wrap him in unbleached linen
and place him in the pine container,
and recite the prayer of forgiveness
for touching him so.

To the Woman Who Killed My Brother

When you struck my brother
with your Mercedes, as he was adorned
in running shorts, anointed

in his own sweat—blood pulsing,
heart quickening, breath laboring,
his whole body in motion—early

May morning, blossom season, smell
of lilac—at first I didn't want to know
your name, the color of your eyes,

because I can never know who you were
before this event entered our lives, this
accident, how you turned a corner

at the light and a life was stopped,
as it will stop forever, this death
you will have to live with.

It could happen to anyone. Impossible
to pay complete attention, one slight
distraction—you turn a corner

and a runner listening to music—
classical—on his iPod, is sprinting
across the street—early Saturday

May morning, blossom season, smell
of lilac, his whole body in motion—
and we can never take it back,

that moment that changed our lives,
that death you will have to live with.
And the sages say: *A transgression*

performed with good intention is better
than a precept performed with evil intention.
And they also say: *We should make ourselves*

holy, and we should be holy, because
on the day of atonement when we beat
our breasts with our fists for the sins

we have committed knowingly and
for the sins we have committed without
thought we do not know who shall live

and who shall die and who shall drive
and who shall be the one driven down—
I say this to you whose name I do not know

and whose anguish I can never imagine.

Twins

Like one nation divided,
the older—by three minutes—bragged:

We had a race, and I won.
The younger would respond:

We had a fight. I punched him out.
Impossible to tell them apart—

in photos, in home movies—
hairy and smooth in equal measures,

matching clothes, thin bodies, freckled,
blue eyes behind black-framed glasses—

as babies, often misidentified—
David, Bruce, Bruce, David—

our parents stuck tags on their lapels
to tell which was which.

They had their quarrels,
their little Jacobs and Esaus—

always on opposing teams,
besting each other, one-upping

for the grade, the sweet words,
the larger portion of the meat.

Once, they fought in the living room,
wrestling each other down

onto the carpet, until our grandmother
silenced them in Yiddish.

Mirror images, they studied hard
across from each other at the table

our father built for them—
calculus and biology, born geniuses.

More and more they spoke a language—
equations and higher physics,

cellular receptors and threshold responses—
only they understood, washed

as they were in the same fluid,
as if their embryos merged

into their original zygote again.
At the hospital, I saw one brother approach

the other, breathless brother, closer,
stroked his chest, laid his hand there,

wept. Across that distance, one said:
"You have been gracious to me."

The other responded:
"Let what is yours remain yours."

And in that silence, did they call
each other by their rightful names?

What We Own

I followed you down the switchback trail of the Grand Canyon and we slept
    in a crevice, and we own that,

and we own those moments tossing the football in front of 4073 Wyncote
    Road
    until the streetlights snapped on,

and we own the smoke bomb the cops threw at us and a few thousand others
    at the Jefferson Airplane concert, Akron, Ohio, 1972,

and we own the whole country we passed through, all the way to the ocean,
    where we checked into a hotel and you discovered, lying atop Gideon's
    Bible,

a black film canister's worth of weed and half-a-pack of rolling papers,
    and we smoked it, and it was good, unbelieving of our luck,

which we own, and the lunar landscape surrounding our tent in Big Bend,
    Texas,
    and the stars, so clear we could read by them, and did,

and we own *The Godfather—Part 1*—on the big screen of that packed theater
    in Evanston, Illinois, and we own that fear

when we were lost in the Tennessee woods, into the dark, and you followed
    some analytical instinct until we found—lo and behold—a road,

and Bob Dylan, who was ours, and Joan Baez, who was also ours, singing
    "The Times They Are a-Changin'" in the War Memorial,

and watching the Indians—miracle of miracles—beat the New York Yankees
at Yankee Stadium during the 1995 heat wave—that, too, that victory, was
    ours,

and I remember how quiet you sometimes were, and I asked about it, and
    you said
    it's a feeling you get, you don't know how to talk about it, and I'd like
    to think

we own that feeling—how we bested the myths. We didn't become murderer
    and victim. We didn't cheat on the other's birthright.

Oh, my brother of the other world, my brother who perhaps will greet me
    when I arrive at that place prepared for by our father,

who is now joined by his own flesh and blood, which is not blood, which is
    not flesh,
    but bones and perhaps spirit,

which we believe in, like the moon, or the unpredictable Cleveland weather,
    or the way the snow descends on the fallen leaves,

or how the sun glazes them now, for their moment, stirred in the slight wind,
    the same wind that blew the Jerusalem dust in our faces, which we own.

My Brother's Resurrection

It's all about saving a life.
According to Leviticus 9:16,
you should not stand aside
while your fellow's blood
is shed, thus says the Lord,

and so Rashi, our interpreter,
reasons: if a life is in danger,
you must save it. Yet
our law forbids desecration
of the body, and, further,

how can the dead, who
in any case are not obliged
to follow the commandments,
be instructed to save a life?
And, still further, how do we know

if the body is dead, which is,
depending on whom you ask,
when the nose is not breathing
or when the heart is not beating,
which, as anyone can see, his

is, in intensive care
at Hackensack Medical Center—
his chest rising and falling,
his breath surging and receding—
not, it is true, according

to death's strict definition:
"cessation of *spontaneous* respiration,"
but, rather, to the rhythm of the machines,
a prognosis this scientist, this Einstein,
would understand: *Brain death,*

the experts said, the skull severed,
prohibiting the blood flow and
the organs to operate on their own.
I brushed the hairy chest
he inherited from our father, our

father, who he had already joined
in the feast, even as my hand
held his hand, even as I listened
to his heart beating with the hope
he'd wake and stand and dress

and walk out of this place into
a morning mysterious as where,
in fact, he already was, not,
it appears, like Lazarus, who, too,
was a brother. If I had been there,

would he have died? Did someone say:
This illness is not to end in death?
That your brother will rise again?
Because aren't there twelve hours
of daylight? We, too, were weeping.

We, too, were moved to indignation
and distress. I said: *Brother,*
come forth. Yes, he was wrapped

in bandages and a cloth. *Come forth.*
Let's walk out of this hell.

There's a Jewish delicatessen—
corned beef on rye bread,
onion rings and black cherry soda—
and you do, you rise, all three of you,
and, though you are in the other world,

it's you—a sixty-year old widow
with your kidney, a forty-year old trucker
with your liver, and your heart, that
sweetness—in a sixty-six-year-old
grandmother—you, all of you, lift yourselves

out of your graves and walk out.
And your mind? How it probed
in your lab at the medical college?
Isn't that, too, still alive, in the way
the mind's discoveries are fueled by

and fuel other minds, passed-on torches
in the greater Mind's examinations
for solutions? That's what science is,
you taught me, a faith, and whoever believes,
you said with your life, saves the world.

Speaking to the Woman With My Brother's Heart

Here you are again, brother,
right in front of me, the most
essential part of you, your heart,

now carried by a sixty-six-year-old grand-
mother grateful for your death,
I would say, but it would be wrong,

she even apologized, though
unnecessarily, that for her to live,
you had to die, and I told her

you wouldn't die for anyone,
but I'm not sure that's true,
and what you taught us,

through your life, that a heart
is a transferable thing, body
to body, if we believe, as you

believed, in the mind's miracles,
in the way step by step we discover
that of which we are capable:

to give life where there is no life,
and to speak from the heart
is to speak from the source of

what is and isn't yours, or ours.
Will she allow me to place
my hand on her chest so that

I can feel your familiar pulsing?
And, further, will she consent
to my request to rest my ear

against her breast so that I can close
my eyes and imagine the way
I'd hear your steady rhythm

as we lay beside each other
in that small room another life ago?
And, in that dark, will you live again?

three

Garden, Sabbath

We open ourselves up
to the only moment there is—
garden, Sabbath—the extra

stillness of late September,
afterlight of harvest moon,
the earth hanging on like

the last blast of the shofar's
bellowing breath, grief
released, hearts broken

open to the silence, hallowed,
wounded by the year. Doesn't
everyone want to be a bird

again? A heart, before
it dies, balanced
with a feather, floating

its appointed flight?
Wasn't it summer?
Weren't the children shrieking

in the water? Wasn't the wind
some kind of refuge?
There's a place where errors

can turn into mindfulness,
changing us into someone
we could not otherwise

become, paying the deserved
price, penance before forgiveness,
which is grace.

Mating Season

In the partial light of a Sabbath dusk,
according to the wisdom of the ages,
desire flushes our flesh the color the sky is
beyond Hidden Pond.

Towards the marsh
we creep, the chorusing tree peepers,
invisible slivers of sound and sex—

and the red-winged blackbird perched
on a reed-tip, singing to its significant other
cruising a cluster of cattails.

A blue goose directs its three-note honk
toward a specific section of sky
and suddenly its mate shapes itself out of the distance,

long neck like a taut chord pulling
down toward the surface, wings stretched stiff and skidding
in a flutter of water.

Season of budding,
of gathering insects in evening mist,
of deer tails disappearing through trees
like feathers floating from a great white bird,

the hermit thrush, the woodcock blasting out
of its tall grasses in a sudden rush and screech,

its needled beak spiraling across the sky towards courtship,
wings whistling—

our yearly pilgrimage to the new season,
the pussy willows you said
your father would gather for your mother,

his message to signal spring's arrival.

Once, after they thought all you children
were in a deep sleep, they snuck off
through the dark woods and down the slope
to the famous swimming hole of Hickory Creek.

They skinnied down to their essential selves
and baptized each other beneath the loud stars.

That's the kind of story that stays with you,
half-a-century later. You will recite it
to our children, hoping they will recite it
to theirs. It's about magic, I guess,

and how a certain kind of love sinks
down, immerses itself, and rises up again.

The Phillip Sparrow

The sparrow's most common call is a short and incessant
chirp. It also has a double call note *phillip* which originated
the now obsolete name of "phillip sparrow."

www.treknature.com

"Without question the most deplorable event in the history
of American ornithology was the introduction of the English
Sparrow." (*The Birds of Ohio*, 1903)

www.sialis.com

I'm told not to love you,
racketing the little blue house
on the sweet gum tree meant

for bluebirds—tramp and hoodlum,
you must go, non-native, weed
of the air, introduced to rid us

of insects, a pest yourself,
breeding in horse droppings,
garbage, barns filled with grain

until it was declared: let them all
be killed and so children smashed
the eggs for hard candy, but

you're too frisky, conspicuous
nuisances, refusing to be eradicated,
deplorable, overrunning our cities,

driving out our songbirds,
dropping your waste everywhere,
breeding in all seasons, each day

eating half of your weight—
even bird lovers hate you,
even the homesteader Bob

who now sits under your perch
and eats his granola bar and says:
I should strangle its throat, still—

namesake, oh you for whom
no law protects: I, too, am a stranger,
I, too, have bred into me a persistence.

Speaking of Miracles

for Mary Lou Brunner and Richard Steigerwald

My friend's wife is dying of cancer.
He's gardening at twilight, scraping
the weeds, telling me about the frog's
calm stare. He says: *The doctor told me:*

"incurable," and I said now tell me
about a miracle. He continues: *Enough already.*
We have an addition to build. We have
a fence to mend. Staring into the garden

bursting with growth. *Hoeing corn*
is healing, he says, working the soil,
his gestures filled with their future feast,
staying alive in the single moment.

Perhaps it's a mistake to think
we have a home, even as we work
in the perennial dusk, even as
our children dress like princesses

and prance around the porch. Perhaps
it's wrong to think of the moment
as ours, the soft after-rain of air,
the sweetness of the Madonna lilies,

the sleep our bodies ease themselves
into, the dreams we trust to the dark—

maybe it's our failure all along,
how the tomatoes will taste

in August, and the corn, our error,
and, again, that harvest, our desire,
where we've hidden all that
accumulation, all that seasonal drift,

all that pulsing of the earth,
our soil seasoned with ancestral bones.
In this blessing we call time, we speak
of the blue moon and flight,

of lips sweet as grape's blood,
wind in our voices. We speak
of this fleeting world, inadequate
to the moment, of fresh pesto

from just-picked basil, mixed
with garlic, asiago cheese, pine nuts,
close as we come to eating the earth directly,
taste of soil and last night's rain.

He says: *if there's a miracle, let it be now.*

The Absence That Was the Tree

Two men are cutting the dead maple down,
limbs and branches first, then the trunk
in sections, all the pieces scattered in piles
on the ground out of which it grew.

It's been released from its enormous weight.
It's given us this gift of a new view—
now the hidden church and the woods
across the road can stare back at us

through where it stood and labored hard
to guard our privacy. The regions
of the sky the branches divided have merged
back again into their indistinct whole.

All the nests have come crashing down.
No longer will we hear birdsong
from that particular quarter: it will not
serve as orientation or point of discussion.

We remark about the extra light,
the new distance its absence
will afford, the extra breezes
traveling through the opened gate.

Death is a way of allowing us to see
beyond where the body formerly stood.

But we have come to love that body
more than the space revealed behind it.

All winter long we'll hack the remnants
even smaller so they'll fit our stove,
warming us in its next life. When
it says farewell, it will be as smoke on the air.

At the Nursing Home, My Mother Is Served *Treif*

The attendant places a plate
of sweet potatoes and ham
in front of my mother,

who all her life has kept
kosher, who has separated
the dairy from the meat,

the dishes in separate cupboards,
the silverware in opposite drawers,
all her life she followed

the letter of the law as far
as she was able, lit the candles
as commanded, braided the bread

for the Sabbath, fasted for atonement,
each waking and rising, in honor
of her parents, in accordance

to God's wishes, the words
she memorized, the gestures
she inherited and passed on—

and what is the culmination
of this devotion? Earlier,
in her box-shaped room, the sun

streaming behind her, white hair
strewn across her gaunt face,
she grabbed my arm and implored:

I'm dead. Shaking from an unseen
wind. *You won't forget me?*
Don't forget me, Papa,

our names dissolving, our relation—
mother and child, one body separated
and drifting, the way she drifts now

from the plate set down before her,
her eyes shifting up, then side-to-side,
as if from something unrecognizable.

My Mother Argues with Ecclesiastes

At the Wailing Wall, when she danced
with the dancers—that was her time,
that was her place—she ate and drank

and enjoyed all the good of her labor—
and now, her body struggling each breath
under the purple comforter,

her right hand holding the white sheet,
her mouth slightly open,
her pale cheeks sunken,

her pink gown open at the breasts,
her eyes, delicate as moth wings, closed—
this almost-death-mask,

these last living moments—is it true,
as it comes to pass, that all,
as it says, is emptiness, these words, this effort?—

loving all, trusting few, always having
something in reserve: if she had one,
she needed two, she'd say,

if she had two, she needed three,
the way she wouldn't trust the banks,
a little of her fortune in each,

or her sons, a little of her wisdom
for each, not all for one, not the whole
in one heart, in case it breaks,

and you're left, she'd say, with nothing.
And here I am, a good son,
or trying to be, at her bedside,

reading to her through her Alzheimer's
and her stone-deafness and her dying,
from Ecclesiastes, whom she interrupts

with her characteristic *chutzpah*:
"No, you *schlemiel!*" she shouts,
"The day of death is *not* better than the day of birth!"

"Are you *meshuggah?!*" she continues,
embarrassing me in front of this wise preacher:
"The house of mourning is *not* greater

than the house of feasting!
Have you ever had children?
Have you ever had the blintzes at Corky and Lenny's?

Have you ever heard Jerry Vale's 'O Sole Mio'?
Have you ever drunk four cups of wine on Passover?
Eat, drink and be merry—there we can agree,"

yet with this breath that came to my bones
in her womb I continue to read to her:
Sorrow is better than laughter,

and I know she's ready to sue him,
she's asking for his name and number
in this, the beginning of her ending,

under the purple comforter.
One generation passeth away, I continue:
there is no remembrance of former things;

neither shall there be any remembrance
of things to come, and my mother rises
again to *kvetch*: "Is this man a *putz*?"

"Is he blind? Is not my son"—pointing to me—
"my afterlife?" Her breath is slowing now,
the nurse applying delicately the morphine,

yet she continues: "Can't he see the bone
of my bone? The flesh of my flesh?"
And so will I in fact carry her

with me all the days of my life?
And what will she carry, empty of her body,
the air her sanctuary? Afternoons

we'd nap together, the shade drawn
against the sharp light, and we'd play the game
of who-falls-asleep-first, her assuring

breath, inhaling time, exhaling chance,
under the purple comforter,
arguing with Ecclesiastes, from beginning to end.

The Shank Bone

Our dog swipes the shank bone from the seder plate,
shakes her muzzle from side to side, takes off
through Elijah's door: this roasted symbol of the sacrificial

lamb we offered in The Temple to remember our exile
and commemorate our liberation now clenched
in the jaws of this overgrown golden retriever puppy,

this what we call in Hebrew *zeroah*, meaning "arm,"
meaning how our God outstretched his enormous arm
to help people in our times of aggravation, what

we're undergoing now, the guests arrived, the table
set with plates and wine glasses, *haggadahs* and candles,
bowl of salt water, bowl of roasted eggs, the *charoset*—

our laborious mortar—chopped and set beside the bitter
herbs, what we will mix in with our dog's Alpo once
we can coerce her to give it up, but she's clamping

and sloshing it around her drenched tongue as if
this were the last bone on earth, as if she understood
that this was the original lamb our high Priest chose

when we all put down our weapons and tools to gather
and witness this primordial offering: to assuage our guilt,
to accommodate our primitive desires, to draw nearer

to the source, our surrendering—before the destruction
and therefore absence of our assigned place
so the scholars say we can sacrifice nowhere

until the source returns and now my five-year-old daughter
has tackled our dog in the yard and pulls hard at the bone,
our guests approaching closer in mesmerized silence.

At My Grandparents' Grave

We did not arrive like the old sages
for advice or to get inspiration
to make the journey to the promised

land. They are not floating above us,
his beard and black coat and long
white *tallis* swirling like a magic scarf

through the blue air, she beautiful
as Bella Chagall with her purple dress
and outstretched arms and thin body

shaped like a swan's. He is not
carrying her off above the town
and his face is not turned impossibly

around so he can stare into her eyes,
his lips on her lips. We did not arrive
to be blessed by the original ancestors

or as inheritors of their great tradition
or to remind ourselves that our lives
should be lived in holiness.

We came—my mother and I—
in the mud of mid-March, rain spraying
out of a gray sky, to mumble what

we remembered of the mourner's prayer
and to place a small stone on their stone.
And to remember them in this life—

how he came home in his fedora hat
exhausted from peddling scrap, how
she *kibitzed* in the kitchen, sewing

buttons on a dress—how we traveled
to this specific ground, where
we can visit them here instead

of there, burned or flaked, ashes
the wind scatters, part of the air,
the dark, the unsettled dust.

At the Synagogue Rummage Sale
During Holocaust Remembrance Day

Basement, Butler, Pennsylvania, the gentiles bargaining
for old *tallises*, worn yarmulkes, a torn *challa* cover, a stained torah,
a hundred thumbed copies of *Anne Frank*—

I walk out and past a circle of bat mitzvah-aged girls
and our rabbi, who stops me and asks if I'll join
in the ritual reading of the victims' names—

each child-turning-into-an-adult attempting to articulate
all those Polish consonants: last name, first name, where from,
when died, what concentration camp—around and around we
    read

the only letters left of those for whom there is no memory,
washed ashore from the other side of our speech, all of our objects
discounted downstairs. We mumble into the dusty air

our mispronunciations. And what does it mean
for a child, in some absurd future,
to attempt to sound the name of a perished life?

Does one soul carry the weight of the other soul?
Does the name belong to both sides of the unknown?
To pronounce a Polish name takes a bit of time,

some stuttering, some silence, the knowledge of faltering,
and you do falter, but you speak it through to the end
in this ritual of commemoration until each student

has spoken all the names on their Xeroxed page—
and the rabbi's voice chants, over the bargainers, the *Kaddish*,
for all of those who have no one to say *Kaddish*.

At Auschwitz-Birkenau

To write poetry after Auschwitz is barbaric.
Theodor Adorno

No poetry in the railroad track
that starts at the welcome center
and ends at the crematorium,

in the barbed wire sectioning off
the tall grasses of the flowering mustard
and clover and violets—nothing

planted, everything wild, nothing touched,
everything as it was, chimneys
without their barracks, red-brick stacks

rising out of the earth as if to filter smoke
from a fire raging under the ground,
the mid-summer, mid-afternoon sun blazing

as if it could torch this all away. No
poetry in the one barrack still intact,
still displaying the date of its construction:

1942, the pine two by fours nailed
at right angles, the rows of holes dug
into the floor for toilets, the dark odors

and dust swirls, the laser-beams of light
shafting through the narrow slats,
the claustrophobic triple-deck beds—

eight to a bunk, the dirt floors, the rats
carrying the diseases, the Polish words
scrawled on the cracked concrete wall:

Keep clean. No talking. No poetry
in the central yard across which husbands
and wives would search through

barbed wire for each other's eyes.
None. Or in the monument to the victims,
boulders falling into each other, plaques

in fifty languages bearing the same message
about how this place is a cry of despair
and a warning. No poetry

in the sixty-five years that passed
since they were kicked out of cattle cars
and hauled past where I stand now,

close enough to brush my shoulders,
marching through the air
my body now inhabits, filing one

after another and stepping down
into the large stomach of the crematorium
that was exploded by its creators

but you can still see the space inside
where they last breathed—no poetry
in the black swamp the chips

of their bones and ashes of their flesh
ended up in, where I am startled
by the glassy eyes of the green frog

that gazes up at me from the bank,
the crouched body stock-still like
the one my daughter pointed

my attention toward near our pond at home.
We'd pause for the screech and leap.
This one screeches.

It leaps.
No—it splashes among the blessed shards—
poetry.

Our Jerusalem

Next Year in Jerusalem

Where was that place?

Was it on the tree-lined street
we drove down Sunday mornings
to look at mansions?

Was it on the basement shelf,
too high for me to reach
to see what was stored there?

Or was it like that horse
that cantered across the white fields
when no one was watching?

Or like the word *death*
I thought about in bed
after my mother whispered the story

and my body shook
and she explained it's a place
we all go?

Would it be next year?

Or perhaps it was like
that diagram she drew
when I asked how I was born:

the man's part,
then the woman's:
This goes into this.

When would I understand?
Next year?
In Jerusalem?

On Passover
she gave me a piece
of rock candy to suck on

as we sat through the Seder—
the sugared cherry sweet
on my tongue as we sounded the words:

Next year in Jerusalem, mine,
she said, as God commanded,
forever.

Planting Trees

In Hebrew school,
on the teacher's desk,
the blue and white *tzedakah* box,
its map of the holy land beside the words:
"Your direct link to the land of Israel."
Between the aleph and the bet
we're told to slip our loose change
into the slot.
We're planting trees.
How many will I own?
A few for my birth,
a few for my manhood,
a few for my marriage,
a few for my death.
A small forest
in a country they say is mine.

Tourists

We travel past hurriedly, comfortable
in our tourist bus, behind sunglasses
and cameras, curious about the F 15's
making designs in the sky.

But aged men and women kneel face down,
kiss the ground in worship. Secrets
are on their lips and now they can rest
where a promise was kept

inside the stones of antiquity,
among the ruins of amphitheaters,
along the streets of Jerusalem,
where tear-stained prayers

add another layer to the Wailing Wall,
where orthodox request them to join *minyan*.
We need no reminder that this is no museum,
as orange trees emerge: they ripen

generation upon generation, or look down
on Masada from an advantageous cable-car
where it is easy to imagine 960 Jews
burying themselves with one Torah.

And that evening in Haifa,
city above the Mediterranean,
a rainbow formed while hail
fell like manna through a halo.

Sundown on the Dead Sea

You can read a book, they say,

and it's true, it's like relaxing
on a couch of water,

but I'm reading streaks
the clouds of planes script
across the universal blue.

The hills of Jordan
are flamed gold, then orange.

If I float far enough
in their direction,
the other side of the sea,

I'm warned I'll be shot
by men I don't know

on a surface so still
I can slide to the motions
of my own waves, a water

so pure my wrinkles
will be smoothed
and my sores become skin
again.

I am buoyed by the salt
that stings if I'm crazy
to duck my head in but
who wouldn't risk
a moment's blindness
to wash the whole body
in the center of the earth?

This is the lowest below
sea level I'll ever be,
even my grave is higher,

and the secret to the healing
powers is all this silence
as I drift, in the oncoming darkness,

toward enemy territory.

For Emil, My Jordanian Student

Mediterranean among the Midwestern
fair-skinned, he enters my office
from the snow that swirls in pockets,
sits down and says he is sad
because the oranges are not so good,
then he notices the picture of my mother
posing in front of the gold dome of the Al-Aqsa Mosque.

Al-Quds, he says. *Where my father was born.*

"Rachel, She Came to Stop the Tanks"

Rachel Corrie was a 23-year-old peace activist who was killed
on March 16, 2003 when an American-made bulldozer
crushed her as she protested the destruction by the Israeli
government of an Arab house in the Gaza Strip. Below are
fragments from the last emails she sent back home.

from February 7, 2003

An eight year old was shot by an Israeli tank
two days before I got here,
and many of the children
murmur his name to me—Ali.

I have a home. I'm allowed to see the ocean.

Today I walked on top of rubble
where homes once stood.

We are all kids curious about other kids.

from February 27, 2003

And when the bulldozers come and take out
people's vegetable farms and gardens.
What is left for people?

Tell me if you can think of anything.
I can't.
I want to dance to Pat Benatar and have boyfriends.
This is not what I asked for
when I came into the world.

This is not what I meant
when I looked at Capital Lake and said:

"This is the wide world, and I'm coming into it."

from February 28, 2003

I slept on the floor next to the youngest daughter, Iman,
and we shared all the blankets. I helped the son
with his English homework. When I woke up
they were watching Gummy Bears dubbed in Arabic.

I spend a lot of time writing
about the disappointment of discovering,
somewhat first-hand,
about the degree of the evil
of which we are still capable.

from the last email (undated):

Dear Papa—

Let me know if you have any ideas
about what I should do for the rest of my life.

One thing I do to make things easier here
I utterly retreat into fantasies
that I'm in a Hollywood movie or a sitcom
starring Michael J. Fox.

So feel free to make something up,
and I'll play along.

At the Wailing Wall

And that last night, after everyone
in the hotel fell asleep, my mother
led me down the rough stones,
whitened by stars so close

we could touch them, to the square
in front of the Old Temple. She wrote
her message on a scrap of paper,
placed it in a fissure with thousands

of others, forced it in tight
and hoped it would stay. *My secret,*
she whispered, *you write one, too.*
The cracks were crammed

with petitions folded and packed in,
sealing the stones with pleadings
in that puzzle of boulders caulked
with tears and words and breath

whispered into the crevices.
We'd passed through checkpoints,
our bags searched, our bodies
scanned and measured and judged

for that fragment, that chamber
of the original heart, that constellation
of oddly shaped stars fixed
in our shared sky, that calendar

that held all of our next years.
A flock of black-robed figures
requested us to follow them
down the stone steps into

a chamber beneath the wall,
thrusting shadows of books, pulsing
birds, into our quivering palms,
their eyes penetrating our flesh,

an obscure longing for us to take up
their responsive chanting, in that place
her tongue spoke of all her life with promise,
in that language she blessed me in.

Shalom is My Middle Name

What my mother left me with—
the word we should mean
when we say every other word,

the word we want to be more
than a word, the word I carry
tucked between other words,

from my birth to my death,
the word embarrassed
by its public display, preferring

its privacy, perhaps lifting
its first letter then retreating
back into the silence. But

there it is, stamped on my passport,
risking itself each time
it passes through security,

each time it wants to haul
its baggage from one country
to the next. Why, after all

these journeys, does it suddenly
step outside and assert itself,
aware as it is of the separations?

Why—
this hello, this goodbye,
this peace?

Considering a Field

Field of tall daisies, clover, buttercups, hay bales
waiting for the gathering, the occasional ground bird,

dried-out goldenrod stalks, and then nothing else
I could name, poor carrier of words that I am—

wouldn't you want to be an open field with butterflies
floating through you, an elevated field, a field

deer can float their watery shapes through, a field
where, if people gathered, they would be compelled

into silence, their thoughts would run their course
like a spring, they would speak only a few last words

and those words would be about beauty, they would measure
the surrounding trees and think seriously about how small

their bodies, perhaps it would be mid-summer, perhaps
the breeze would chill then flush their skin, perhaps

they would be distracted and forget a little where they were
and be indistinguishable from the daisies, the clover, the buttercups.

Like a Bird Entering Through a Window
and Leaving Through Another Window

Well, I can tell you the tale of the woodpecker's persistence,
the way we can tell time by its tapping throughout the morning,
with or without us, the only-seen-at-a-certain-angle-of-light
gossamer spinning above that field, sparkling in dew-drench
and fog, signifying the season, that no matter what—freezing
rain, more unexpected snow—we have, despite all deceptions,
this turning, this springing, as the willow with its beads from
last night's rain agrees with whatever the swallows are suggesting,
and I can tell you that today I'd really like to be happy,
and that, because we disappear, we want a singular life,
what with the full day-moon and deep lilacs, the afterworld
to consider, not unlike the robin, unobserved save for the singing,
save for the shadows of its nest, the bits of hay it scatters on the wind,
save for the wind, or the soil we become, which is something. And
I can tell you that there's no telling what our deaths make us do—
sermonizing the air, staring into the ripples, anticipating the frogs—
it takes that much faith, it takes that much courage, wondering
if love is a bird perched on the highest limb of the soul. And
I can tell you how every moment reveals our resurrection, and
to wonder what or who allowed us to witness this fog dispersing,
this water, these geese, this willow, is to wonder why the blue jay
would look back to the branch from which it sprang into flight,
with so much sky ahead, or to speculate on how a tree's shadow
is devoted to the tree, until dark descends and they both disappear
into a larger devotion, that place behind the ribs, where we carry
each person we love for the rest of our lives. And though

we'll never be free of our grief, the fat rhododendron's purple
is still drenched by the rain that woke us into love, how the world
happens, by happenstance or design, that the candle burning
all night and into the morning still burns doubled in the window.
So let me tell you that we're nothing, unless you believe, as I do,
that the soul travels from body to body, and so we must fill that soul
with beauty, and truth, and that as it came in it goes forth, like
a bird entering through a window and leaving through another window,
and that our lives are an allowance for that soul to sing, sweetly, if it can.

four: The Torah Garden

—for Ganya

The Torah Garden

I sound the shofar for the New Year
and in this suspended time,
my life is focused in my mouth,
lips on the ram's horn I purchased in Jerusalem,
rending the air with its broken notes,
summoning us to renounce:

fashion a kingdom, it says,

open yourselves up to the only moment there is—
this stillness,
this garden hanging like the last blast of its bellowing breath.

*

Here we don't watch the debates,
rather these maples and oaks absorbing the last of their light,
burning the leaves into our raptures.

We know the consuming issues.
We don't need the spin-doctors.

Rather the many-jeweled apple tree,
its bedecked burden of giving itself up all at once to the dark.

Here we don't follow the scandals,
only silence that like this new snow sweeps and accumulates
without reason, each flaking into its own distance,
all morning and into the evening across the wide expanses
of the immediate territories.

There is no rationale in how moments steady themselves
and begin to take on the form of a life.

Chimes articulate the soul visible on the air, an inaudible scale,
a dust-like confusion, ungraspable logic,

the way I can't stop this gabbing about our exile,
the days, we're told, when we're beclouded in mind
and singularly wounded, without doctrine, chaotic, unsound in
        interpretation,
and perhaps we are, we're seeds the wind willy-nilly uplifts,

forgetful of our task, unfocused in our attention, unable to
contemplate the divine chariot

and the emanations.

*

Late afternoon on a Saturday,
designated the day of rest
and so this writing is a sin
against the deep powers of silence.

It's difficult to think of transgression
on a day so full of early spring
four ducks splash-landed on the pond
and the daffodils are lifting their trumpets,
announcing their bursting.

No rest for the robins,
who gather their twigs and bits of grass,
none for the lettuce seeds under grow lights—
already thrusting their green spears through soil—
certainly no respite for the laborious pounding of my heart
as I spy you dressing in a circle of sunlight,
your flesh flushed by the love we've just made,
according to some commandment.

*

The world acquires flavor only when a little
of the other world is mingled with it—

so I borrow Rick's beat-up uninsured rusted-out truck
and shake and bump my way to Watson's horse farm
where Jack the owner barks back his huge Rottweiler
then climbs up into his front loader and gestures
with his tanned left arm out the window for me to follow
toward the small mountain of manure, motioning for me
to back up and I have to force the shift into reverse, Jack
lowering the loader's claw into the steaming pile and lifting it,
steam curling as if just removed from an oven. I position
the truck. The black magic rains into the bed—
one, two, three loads, all this junker will hold.
Fiddling with the country stations, I pull out
and onto Scrubgrass Road, hauling our new earth
pulsing with the ingredients of creation.

    *

Like the Torah,
for everything is in it,
we turn and turn and turn over the rocky soil,

haul water from the pond in drywall buckets,
rake leaves, gather branches, toss hay onto the potatoes—
dank wet earth for them to root down in,
light filtering through the lilacs.

You pick and bite the top of a garlic leaf,
hand it to me, our longings
like twigs in the beak of a swallow in flight,
the garden in ascension, blossoms on the strawberries.

*

The birch we planted sways slightly,
its one branch thin almost as air,
yet a swallow suddenly appears, perches,
observes the day. What was nothing
is now a shape growing skyward
and a rest for birds and a small shade
for the grass that burns by afternoon.

And the Chinese willows we cultivate
for our daughters' arrivals
spin out their twisted yellow branches
toward the water that nourishes them.

Here, what was not here.

This house, according to our vision.

These bodies, because we decide,
moment by moment, to keep them.

*

Our daughters step off the bus and charge full tilt across
the sweetness of the fresh-seeded hayfield
toward the blossoming dogwood.

Moses had his Sinai and we have the brief life of this dogwood,
which, if it weren't so alone among the maples and oaks,
if it weren't so embarrassed by its beauty,
perhaps we wouldn't be so distracted like those two geese racketing
    up the sky—
if the breeze weren't so soft across the familiar skin of our faces,
if the spring itself weren't so unreliable in its arrivals and departures,
perhaps something could be said,
something simple could announce itself and the evening
would unfold like any other, useful and dignified,
disappearing into wherever the dogwood leaves disappear into.

Moses had his burning bush and we have our dogwood.
Would he trade his dividing of the great sea for these children,
parting the clover in their abandon?

His slow tongue for their dogwood song?

    *

So will it come to pass?
Will we receive rain in its season,
the former rain and the later rain?

Will the ground produce its fruit?
Will we gather in the corn, the broccoli, the carrots, the peas, the
      beans, the squash,
the potatoes, the onions—the red and the white and the gold—
the tomatoes of every designation, the peppers?

The labor of laying down all the seeds,
laying them down like all the words scribbled into the book of a life.

      *

You do not count on this abundance,
but all winter long you consulted the texts, ordered the seeds,
dusted the grow lights, began again the plotting of what goes
    where—
every year you hold true to your imagined Eden.

You tilled the soil, planted the seed, weeded and watered,
cultivating your obligations to the earth.

Swallowtails surveyed the tassels.

Wind every-so-often reopened its song.

And the poems I wrote were full of loss, but of loss with grace,
in the shadow of a willow—we were finding our way into a rhythm,
recalling who we were: June, after all,
what you wanted to hold onto,
roses against the redbrick, poppies soft as tissues,
strawberries fully red and hidden in the unmown grasses,
the mock orange spreading its white blossoms over the porch
    swing—

when the petals drop, the children call them: *warm snowflakes*—

June, season of tomato stakes and tossing straw onto the potatoes,
hard green apples and blueberries and grapes shaping themselves,
the flowering blackberries proliferating along the field's edge—

and, late afternoons, the sun rounding the sky's absolute blue,
the garden layered in shadow,
the children splashing their thin bodies against the heat—

you pause,

hands resting on the handle of your hoe,
the sweat of your body's labor sweetening the air,
and allow yourself the distraction that, perhaps, yes:
it's all one continuous blossoming,
these cells that everywhere sing their pulsing songs, your life.

      *

And so Tolstoy was wrong:
families are not all happy in the same way.

That the juice packed inside is also ours,
that it will sweeten our tongues until our next language,
the blueberries so abundant we grasp them by the handfuls,
discrete and delicious and without damage,
producing long after we unpin the netting and leave what remains
for the birds that will plunder until they themselves are gone.

Only the frost will stop them now, proliferating until summer
    itself perishes,
according to the instructions of However-Long-the-Light-Lasts.

I eat the fruit of your seeds, torahs in my mouth, dwelling in the
    devouring flame,
in this garden where we allow wildness its portion:

the bat with the injured wing crawling slow as a second hand up
    the spruce,
stuttering one step at a time, pausing high above our heads
and turning, facing us in its ascension:

Keep yourselves holy, because I am holy.

     *

Are the orthodox in black coats forever burning their bodies?

Butterfly bush, sustain me, hydrangeas, release me
into the honeysuckle air
of late afternoon silence and the search for shadows, any shadow,
any gathering place for coolness, any weeping willow near any
    water,
any breeze that would carry the dream forward,
the one about childhood and its earnest return.

Yellow finch nervous in yellow sunflower,
flighting from leaf to leaf, kissing the seeds.

It's not for me to wonder what makes up this moment:
my daughters clipping the retriever's unruly blonde fur on the
    front porch,
carefully guiding the clippers across the enormous golden back,
mats tumbling out in monumental clumps, my daughters laughing,
    the heat rising.

It's not for me to wonder why Rabbi Bonan of Pshkiske wrote the
    same page every day and every evening he burned it.

   *

And perhaps the Kabbala was right: it's all a tending, a holding
      onto lightly, a deeper in,
a flighting and forgetting, a carrying forth, an unfolding.

The rabbi said to his son: *I will give you ten coins if you tell me*
      where God is.
The son replied: *I will give you twenty to tell me where he is not.*

In the wheelbarrow overloaded with weeds?
In the sunflowers drooping? In the apples wormed-through?

Won't we be judged for the pleasures foregone in this life?

Shouldn't we wax elegiac and keep silence in our souls and noth-
      ing in our pockets,
open to every occasion, measuring our capacity for happiness,
the wren in the willow, the red-winged blackbird in the tip-top of
      the maple, singing:
compost, compost?

    *

Among the rotten and the decayed, the spoiled and the decomposing,
where skunk and raccoon feast, among the leftovers and garden
    remnants,
the sweet and the stale, the melon rinds and the tomato skins,
all the year's leftovers—bruised apples and torn corn sheaves,
where flies and worms celebrate: I stake my claim,
with shovel and spud bar and post-hole digger, tape-measuring
each hole I've been digging myself down into, two feet under,
below the frost line—here, I'll plant six locust posts:

"four dollars a piece," Jake Byler said, in the grove behind his house,
between a cornfield and a bean field, all sweat and sawdust,
chain-sawing and hauling them over: "and they'll last seventy years."

Locust posts for the compost bin, I sang to myself, as we loaded them
    onto the truck.

    *

After we're gone, you say,
our shadows stretched against the tilled soil,
we'll push up a tree together.

      *

I want to be a harp for your songs,
wind through the field's tall grasses, shadows of pear trees,

I want to be your instrument of silence as you whistle through
     your tasks,
in your comings in and in your goings out.

I wish that writing your garden were as easy
as the mourning dove makes it seem,
singing its repetitive five notes with just the right cadence,
pausing before beginning again, a chant
as tedious as the passages of the Torah we train ourselves to recite
     week after week.

And who is the rabbi of the rain,
and who understands his sermon,
and who are the prophets of the wet earth?

And who is this chronicler of the Holy of Holies,
tall and thin, bearded and established,
white ear-locks, cap pinned to white hair,
black eyes squinting at the parchment as if into a door he could
     open,
his hand inscribing precisely as if stitching skin to skin?

Now his fixed attention is tracing the script
that will be chanted before the people for another century:

the agonies and the dream visions,
the prognostications and the hidden wisdoms and buried codes
        and wonders and correspondences—

flesh into fire, bones into prophecies.

        *

I will make it a possession for the porcupine,

or, in our case, the raccoon, who nest in the barn loft,
who are resting now and waiting for the corn's ripening,
who each night avoid the trap with its cracker and peanut butter
and instead tear down the trashcan and scatter its remnants,
and so we retrieve the ancient paint-stained boom box
and extension cord, search through static for a rough music,
antenna directed at the stars, a hip-hop-talk-jive-rap
that will stun these beasts out of the stalks, a battalion
of percussion that will blast them back to their bivouacs,
a barrage of talk and backtalk that will turn them away
from these laborious fruits:

and so the first-born of the poor shall feed,
and the needy shall lie down in safety.

*

"I only give these to those I love," you say,
passing out the raspberries, those tiny roses.

You picked them,
between moonset and sunrise,
the guests still sleeping, filling your basket.

*I take the sweetness of thy name
into my mouth for sustenance.*

    *

According to the laws of soil and rain,
sunlight and luck and the gardener's attention,
all summer long the sunflowers grew,
taller than our heads, taller than our house,
so tall the farmers looked up briefly
from their tractors and manure spreaders,
and we crouched under leaves large as tabletops,
large as living rooms, large as the hearts of saints.

September holds its own,
rustlings and the flushed inevitabilities of desire,
the outer garment of an inner necessity.

Migrating birds, what wisdom?

Speak of the tomatoes' meat and the full moon,
the dance tent, of lips sweet as grapes' blood,
the sauce simmering in the bright kitchen,
our days untucked like the beds we never completely make,

the late afternoon sun gleaming the oak of the Amish table,
the garden melons sliced into crescent moons
and set beside the white hydrangeas.

Our offerings are offerings of fire,
our bodies the bread the earth will eat.

*

There's a tree within the tree the light reaches deeper into—

Time for awe and the seasonal decay, for penitents to sway like
    these leaves
in the broken wind, for casting off the withered heart,
for the swallows to float toward the next chronicler, the days
    equipped for flight.

I climb the ladder for the last of the apples,
higher and higher with the thought of cider,
picking each within reach,
stepping out onto the thinnest branches for the difficult ones,
the obscure ones, the ones concealing themselves in their dark
    clusters of leaves—
forgetting the height, how close my death—their devotion,
to blossom and therefore fall and be part of the larger earth.

Not like Frost, not overtired,
I shake the limbs into the green hail-swirl.
Bella, six and in the flush of her enthusiasms,
chases and gathers and tosses them into the wheelbarrow,
the summer-into-autumn sun perched on the dusk-side of the tree.

It's the day of atonement.
Will we be inscribed in the book?
Will we find a way to live?
Will we have a place to store our griefs?

This is not a synagogue
and we are not beating our breasts,
our sins spread out like this fruit we'll simmer into sauce,
in this harvest we desired.

    *

...and so I sound the shofar for the New Year,
and in that suspended time,
my life is focused on my mouth,
lips on the ram's horn I purchased in Jerusalem,
rending the air with its broken notes,
summoning us to thin ourselves out, to renounce:

*

Fashion a kingdom, it says.

Acknowledgments

Much thanks to the editors of the journals and anthologies where the following poems first appeared (sometimes in different versions and titles):

Brevity: "At the Nursing Home, My Mother Is Served *Treif*"

Chautauqua: "Job Description," "Three-Card Monte"

Connotation Press: "A History of America," "Furnace and Shrine"

Controlled Burn: "Speaking of Miracles," "Like a Bird Entering Through a Window and Leaving Through Another Window" (as "Lecture to a Creative Writing Class")

Connecticut Review: "The birch we planted sways slightly..." (as "After a Friend's Suicide")

The Cortland Review: "You do not count on this abundance..." (as "One Continuous Blossoming")

Enskyment: "Speaking of Miracles," "The Shank Bone"

5 AM: "Mating Season" (as "Your Parents' Baptism")

The Fourth River: "Speaking to the Woman With My Brother's Heart," "Two Geese," "The Last Torah Reader"

Image: "Twins," "At the Synagogue Rummage Sale During Holocaust Remembrance Day"

Lake Effect: "At the Wailing Wall" (as "Our Majestic Season")

The Laurel Review: "Considering a Field"

The Mid-American Review: "What We Own"

Poetrymagazine.com: "Among the Unspoken Names," "Lobsters"

Prairie Schooner: "Garden, Sabbath," "At My Grandparents' Grave," "At Auschwitz-Berkenau"

Sampsonia Way: "Oil City Serenade"

Tifferet: "Late afternoon on a Saturday..." (as "Keeping the Sabbath Holy")

West Branch: "Think of David and His Pleadings," "There's a tree within a tree..." (as "Apple-Picking With My Daughter on the Days of Awe")

Voices de la Luna: "The Accident," "Washing My Brother's Body," "To the Woman Who Killed My Brother," "My Brother's Resurrection"

The Working Poet: "11:11"

Zeek Magazine: "Our Jerusalem" (as "Education of an American Jew"), "The Shank Bone"

I want to thank my friends Scott Minar, Ann Pancake, and Dan Roche for their support and invaluable assistance in the creation of this manuscript. I'm grateful to the folks at Autumn House Press, and am particularly fortunate to know and work with Michael Simms and Richard St. John. Much gratitude to Miriam and Bella, for their laughter and wisdom. Finally, deep thanks to the poet behind these poems, muse and editor, torah and garden—Christine Hood.

The Autumn House Poetry Series

Michael Simms, General Editor

• Winner of the annual Autumn House Poetry Prize

▲ Hardcover

Design and Production

Cover and text design by Chiquita Babb

Interior photograph: iStockphoto

Cover photographs: iStockphoto

Author photograph: Bella Terman

Text set in Truesdell, a font designed by Steve Matteson in 1994, based on the original design drawn by Frederic Goudy in 1930

Printed by McNaughton & Gunn on 55# Glatfelter Natural